E.
PERSPECTIVES FROM THE FIELD

Case Examples to Accompany:
Introduction to Social Work and Social Welfare:
Empowering People
Ninth Edition

EMPOWERING PEOPLE
PERSPECTIVES FROM THE FIELD

Case Examples to Accompany:
Introduction to Social Work and Social Welfare: Empowering People
Ninth Edition

Edited By Charles Zastrow
George Williams College

THOMSON
BROOKS/COLE

Australia • Brazil • Canada • Mexico • Singapore • Spain
United Kingdom • United States

© 2008 Thomson Brooks/Cole, a part of
The Thomson Corporation. Thomson, the
Star logo, and Brooks/Cole are trademarks
used herein under license.

Thomson Higher Education
10 Davis Drive
Belmont, CA 94002-3098
USA

ALL RIGHTS RESERVED. No part of this work covered by the copyright hereon may be reproduced or used in any form or by any means—graphic, electronic, or mechanical, including photocopying, recording, taping, Web distribution, information storage and retrieval systems, or in any other manner— except as may be permitted by the license terms herein.

Printed in the United States of America

1 2 3 4 5 6 7   10 09 08 07 06

Printer: West Group

978-0-495-10465-0
0-495-10465-5

For more information about our products, contact us at:
Thomson Learning Academic Resource Center
1-800-423-0563

For permission to use material from this text or product, submit a request online at
http://www.thomsonrights.com.
Any additional questions about permissions can be submitted by email to
thomsonrights@thomson.com.

Empowering People:
Perspectives from the Field
Edited by Charles Zastrow

This website/booklet illustrates with case examples how social workers can empower: individuals, families, groups, organizations, and communities. An additional case example illustrates how to empower people through making legislative changes.

This website/booklet is intended to be used with the text *Introduction to Social Work and Social Welfare: Empowering People*, 9th edition (published by Thomson Brooks/Cole, 2008, Belmont, CA). The case examples are designed to correspond with the chapters in Part II "Social Problems and Social Services" of the text. (Part I of the text is entitled "Introduction: Social Welfare and Social Work." The three chapters in this introductory section of the text have some case examples that also illustrate empowerment.)

The 14 chapters in Part II of the text are entitled:

Chapter 4:	Poverty and Public Welfare
Chapter 5:	Emotional/Behavioral Problems and Counseling
Chapter 6:	Family Problems and Services to Families
Chapter 7:	Sexual Orientation and Services to GLBT Individuals
Chapter 8:	Drug Abuse and Drug Treatment Programs
Chapter 9:	Crime, Juvenile Delinquency, and Correctional Services
Chapter 10:	Problems in Education and School Social Work
Chapter 11:	Work-Related Problems and Social Work in the Workplace
Chapter 12:	Racism, Ethnocentrism, and Strategies for Advancing Social and Economic Justice
Chapter 13:	Sexism and Efforts for Achieving Equality
Chapter 14:	Aging and Gerontological Services
Chapter 15:	Health Problems and Medical Social Services
Chapter 16:	Physical and Mental Disabilities and Rehabilitation
Chapter 17:	Overpopulation, Misuse of the Environment, and Family Planning

For each of these chapters one case example is presented in this booklet. (For two of the chapters, chapter seven and seventeen, two case examples are presented.)

Empowerment in social work practice is the process of helping individuals, families, groups, and communities increase their personal, interpersonal, socioeconomic, and political strength and develop influence toward improving their circumstances. Much of what social workers do is focused on empowering people.

A major focus of these case examples is an interactive "critical thinking" experience for both students and instructors. Instructors are encouraged to have their students read the case examples and then discuss and reflect on the critical thinking questions at the end of each case example. The case examples are now presented.

Table of Contents

                                                                             PAGE

Poverty and Public Welfare
Coordinated Community Response to Aid Low-Income Families   5

Emotional/Behavioral Problems and Counseling
Empowerment of a Client and Her Family   9

Family Problems and Services to Families
Counseling a Woman Who is a Victim of Domestic Abuse   14

Sexual Orientation and Services to GLBT Individuals
Group Therapy with Non-Offending Parents of Sexually Abused Children   18
Empowering a Young Male to Confront His Sexual Curiosity and to Terminate His Sexual Misconduct   22

Drug Abuse and Drug Treatment Programs
Motivational Enhanced Therapy for a Person with a Drug Addiction   26

Crime, Juvenile Delinquency, and Correctional Services
Parole Services for an Individual with Multiple Criminal Convictions   30

Problems in Education and School Social Work
Support Groups at School for Young Girls Who are Living in Families with Spousal Abuse   35

Work-Related Problems and Social Work in the Workplace
Improving Morale in an Organization   38

Racism, Ethnocentrism, and Strategies for Advancing Social and Economic Justice
Empowering a Hmong Client to Make Positive Changes   42

Sexism and Efforts for Achieving Equality
Changing Domestic Violence Legislation   46

Aging and Gerontological Services
Using "Validation" and "Reality Orientation" with a Person
with Dementia   **49**

Health Problems and Medical Social Services
Extended Family Therapy for Stress-Impacted Youth   **52**

Physical and Mental Disabilities and Rehabilitation
Empowering an Individual with Cerebral Palsy   **56**

Overpopulation, Misuse of the Environment, and Family Planning
Empowering a Client to Make a Decision   **59**
Empowering a Pregnant Sixteen-Year-Old Teenager and
Her Parents   **65**

Chapter 4: Poverty and Public Welfare

Coordinated Community Response to Aid Low-Income Families
James P. Winship, MSW, DPA

Credentials:

Associate Professor in a University Social Work Department

Case Example:

In keeping with his campaign promise to "end welfare as we know it," President Clinton in August, 1996 signed the Personal Responsibility and Work Opportunities Reconciliation Act (PRWORA), a comprehensive overhaul of the existing welfare system, ending 60 years of guaranteed federal assistance with far-reaching implications for poor families, communities, states, and for social work and human services. As part of the welfare reform, each state had the freedom to design its own public assistance system. Wisconsin, under the leadership of then-Governor Tommy Thompson, was one of the most aggressive states in reforming welfare. Wisconsin Works (W-2), the Wisconsin program, was an aggressive work-first program, in which benefits were only given after applicants had repeatedly demonstrated that they were unable to find work. In Wisconsin, there was an 85 percent drop in the welfare rolls, from 35,000 families in early 1997 to 6700 in 1999.

One of the counties in Wisconsin where the welfare rolls plummeted most drastically was a county located on the Southeastern border with Illinois, with a population of 152,000. Two cities comprise almost two-thirds of the county's population. One city has pockets of poverty and one of the highest teen pregnancy rates in the country.

In April 1997, a broad array of county service providers and advocates were concerned about the effects W-2 was having on recipients, and on local resources. One of the issues was the policy of "light touch," in which recipients were not told about available supports (like subsidized child care) unless they specifically asked for the supports/services. These providers and advocates met to share their concerns and organize the "County W-2 Response Team."

In December 1998, the group changed its name to the Poverty Response Team (PRT) in recognition of the fact that comparatively few families were left on W-2 and that many former recipients are still struggling. A social work professor (that would be me) at a nearby university was elected as chairperson of the group.

By 1999, the number of persons on public assistance had declined so greatly that counties were allowed to disperse unused funds to community service agencies that were serving clients that were W-2 eligible. This Community Reinvestment was considered "one-time in nature."

When Community Reinvestment funds became available, the PRT began a six-month planning process. The social work professor, who had experience in other community planning efforts, suggested a broad community-based approach for identifying priority issues and collaborative responses. This process was approved, and an invitation went out to social service agencies, advocacy groups, and churches to participate in the planning.

In two meetings, nine areas were identified as top priorities for low-income working families: housing, transportation, childcare, parenting/family counseling, literacy, mental health/AODA, client advocacy, employment-related expenses, and Individual Development Accounts. Individual Development Accounts (IDAs) provide incentives for the working poor population to save money for specified purposes such as retirement or home ownership. In the plan, the state or federal government helps low income individuals set up accounts in a financial institution and then matches the amount each individual puts into the account. IDAs are modeled somewhat after the individual retirement account system that tends to benefit more affluent citizens.

Work groups were formed from the Poverty Response Team members to address each area. The work groups then reported back to the full Poverty Response Team at a later meeting. After listening to the specifics from each work group, the Team agreed to narrow its focus and pursue the preparation of an umbrella proposal for Community Reinvestment funds.

Despite the fact that the turn-around time between the Community Reinvestment Request for Proposal's formal release and the due date was extremely short, PRT submitted multi-agency initiatives for housing, utilities and debt reduction, transportation, and food assistance programs. The bulk of the proposals were funded. This group of committed service providers resulted in the expenditure of $1.7 million. Moreover, this process afforded smaller communities in the county the leverage to access funds they would not have otherwise had.

One area in which the Community Reinvestment funds were well used was in the area of transportation. Four agencies in the two cities and one small town in the northern part of the county jointly submitted the transportation part of the proposal and implemented the program once funded. Monies were used for bus tokens and car repairs. One example of a beneficiary of the program was Lynette Fox (names have been changed.) Ms. Fox, a single parent, was severely ill with pneumonia when she began to have troubles paying the rent. Unfortunately, Ms. Fox reported that her car was "starting to show its age" at this time. Since she had no family in the area, and there was no public transportation in her small town, it was essential to have a working car in order for her to see a doctor and to travel to her job, some fifteen miles away. Through the funds, her car received the needed repairs. Ms. Fox later reported that without transportation assistance, she would not have been able to get to the physician's office in order to receive the medical attention needed to regain her health and maintain her employment. Transportation assistance allowed her to continue paying the rent and keep her family under one roof. Without it, she reported, "I would have lost everything."

There were several reasons that the planning process was successful. Many of the service providers and advocates already knew each other before the planning began, and there was a level of trust already established. The planning process was seen as transparent, and social service agencies, especially in smaller communities, did not feel that they were being (or would be) excluded. The chairperson of the group, a social work professor, was seen as an "honest broker," as neither he nor his university would benefit from any of the funding.

As a result of the collaborative effort of applying for Community Reinvestment funds, the number of providers and advocates consistently attending PRT meetings almost doubled, from twenty to close to forty. The Poverty Response Team's collaborative efforts in securing Community Reinvestment funds were praised as a model for other communities in the newsletter of the state's premier advocacy group for low-income families.

The success in gaining Community Reinvestment Funding has given PRT members the confidence that they can be successful in other efforts to aid low-income individuals and families. They have conducted several community awareness campaigns, and currently the PRT is working with bus companies in the two cities to extend the hours of operation, so that individuals without cars can obtain second-shift employment and attend classes at the local technical college.

Questions for Students

In this case example a social worker facilitates a community planning group to improve a variety of services to public assistance recipients (in a program entitled Wisconsin Works, which is Wisconsin's name for its Temporary Assistance to Needy Families program). Describe the specific strategies used by the social worker and the Poverty Response Team to improve services to (and thereby better empower) recipients of Wisconsin Works. Assume you are a member of this Poverty Response Team. What other strategies would you have suggested that this community planning group should have pursued? Would you have included potential recipients (that is public assistance recipients) on this community planning group? Why is it usually advantageous to include potential consumers of services on community planning groups?

Chapter 5: Emotional/Behavioral Problems and Counseling

Empowerment of a Client and Her Family
Patricia Danielson, BASW, CSW

Credentials:

Patricia Danielson, BASW, CSW (Certified Social Worker) in December, 1993 with a Bachelor of Arts Degree in Social Work. She served her 480-hour field placement at a county Human Services Department and has been employed by that agency since February 1994. Currently she is a member of a team that works with children and families where there are issues of sexual abuse, physical abuse, attachment disorder, mental illness and reactive behavioral problems.

Case Example:

There are so many ways in which the generalist social worker empowers clients that the strategies become routine. An opportunity such as this—to prepare a case example where we must take some time to sort out which empowerment strategies we have used with a client family is an extremely valuable method for assessing our practice. Common examples of routine strategies for empowerment are establishing a mutually respectful relationship with the client, working together to determine what services are needed, and developing a plan to help the family access services. We begin to identify the strengths of each family member in order to help them build upon these assets. Clear professional boundaries should be established and we must respect boundaries set by the client. Acceptance of the client and the problem is paramount—we cannot empower if we sit in judgment.

The following case example illustrates a variety of empowerment strategies used with a family in crisis. It should be noted that some of the services provided, especially out of home placements, were not always successful. Nevertheless, the family continued to gain a strong sense of empowerment because they had a voice in determining when a placement should be ended—or when one was needed to interrupt the child's cycle of violent behavior. Names and other identifying details have been changed.

In late October 1993, I was assigned as the Delinquency Team case manager for 13-year-old Jessie Stone; her younger sister, Janie; and their mother, Stella Smith. The family had a prior history with the county agency due to substantiated reports of parental neglect and unfit living conditions. This earlier situation evolved from a period of parental depression, unemployment, and increased alcohol use. A Children's Protective Services (CHIPS) dispositional order was put into effect and resulted in Jessie and Janie being placed in foster care for several months. Stella and her daughters resented the intrusion into their lives by the Court and Human Services and became quite "hostile" toward county workers.

Due to a series of delinquency referrals for "battery" and "disorderly conduct" in the fall of 1993, the case was reopened and Jessie was identified as the primary client. Presenting problems included Jessie's violent outbursts in the home and school environments, her non-compliance with rules and curfew, her use of drugs and alcohol, and Jessie's increasing risk of causing harm to others. In this second quarter of 8th grade Jessie faced expulsion from Middle School due to her verbally and physically violent outbursts in the school environment. Six police referrals were received by the County Intake Department for incidents occurring in October and November of 1998. Jessie was charged with four counts of disorderly conduct and two counts of battery. She was adjudicated delinquent and placed in a group home for adolescent females. Over the next two and a half years, Jessie and her family rode on waves of emotional and behavioral turmoil which were at times so intense that it seemed unlikely she could ever return to the family home.

Out-of-home placements during this time period included two group homes; three extended stays in residential treatment facilities; foster care and respite foster care; numerous short-term stays in juvenile detention and three brief psychiatric hospitalizations. Jessie's mental health diagnoses changed over time as providers gained better insights into Jessie's emotional and behavioral patterns. Initially, she was diagnosed with substance addiction, conduct and intermittent explosive disorders, and she met many criteria for antisocial personality disorder. Later diagnoses focused on treatment for mood disorder/bipolar disorder with psychotic features, posttraumatic stress disorder and borderline personality disorder. At first, Jessie resisted psychiatric treatment due to the stigma of mental illness and, thus, perpetuated her "tough kid" façade in order to avoid hospitalization. Eventually the agency's psychiatrist and I were able to normalize the concept of mental illness for Jessie, and she became more comfortable in requesting medication changes and voluntary hospitalizations. Stella became more trusting and confident as she discovered that she had a voice in determining what forms of treatment were most beneficial to Jessie.

At a dispositional hearing in February 2000, Jessie faced new charges of battery, disorderly conduct and criminal damage to property. These incidents occurred while she was living in structured alternate care environments. Jessie was again adjudicated delinquent and the Court ruled that Jessie be placed in a Type II Correctional CCI (child caring institute), which would serve as the formal conduit for what seemed to be Jessie's inevitable placement at a correctional training school.

Stella Smith was overwhelmed with the task of parenting her volatile and defiant child. Stella's personal support network was extremely limited—she was estranged from her extended family, the girls' father had never been involved in their lives, and Stella did not want to subject her friends to Jessie's tirades. It was Stella's belief that school officials, local law enforcement and Human Services professionals looked down on her and ascribed Jessie's behavior problems to poor parenting. In truth, Stella had numerous strengths as a parent, sole provider and homemaker. It took nearly a full year to develop a fully functioning support network for Stella, Jessie, and Janie. I advocated strongly for the family with law enforcement, placement providers, agency supervisors and intake workers. A plan was developed for Stella to call to schedule appointments only during a specific receptionist's shift; this effectively reduced her frustration over scheduling errors and being told that there were no openings. My supervisors allowed me to choose which agency outreach workers would be assigned to the case, based on their past successes with complex client families.

Underlying issues which emerged over the course of my work with the family were tremendously significant. The Stone and Smith family histories were positive for both substance abuse and mental health disorders. The girls' self-esteem and ability to form relationships had been negatively affected by their father's abandonment. Stella was employed full-time at a low-paying job with no health insurance benefits. And, most significantly, Jessie was a recent victim of rape by several adult males at a "drug house" in her home community, but was unable to talk about it until a year or so afterward. Amid the chaos, 10-year-old Janie Stone took on the role of family guardian. She was generally the first to seek intervention when family tension escalated. Janie would confide in her school guidance counselor who would then contact me. Janie frequently was caught in the middle as her mother and sister each attempted to pull her into their corner. She was emotionally torn, fearful of another breakup of the family and angry because Jessie commanded so much of her mother's energy and attention.

Obstacles to developing working relationships with the family members included the low self-esteem of each individual; their ego defenses of anger, blaming others and verbal aggression; and the use of "splitting" to disrupt or avoid a team approach to service provision. A major obstacle to providing an appropriate plan of care for Jessie was the refusal of officials in the juvenile justice system to differentiate between delinquent/criminal behavior and behaviors which are more appropriately attributed to mental health disorders and/or reactive behaviors of childhood trauma.

The most meaningful forms of empowerment that I used with this family were active listening, advocacy, and helping them to find a voice that would be heard. Their communication styles were extremely aggressive; they yelled, cursed and hurled insults. As a result, people backed away from them and judged them harshly. After several failed meetings, I used a strategy of writing each person's complaints and requests with colored marker on a large piece of butcher paper. This visible evidence that I was listening and recording seemed to calm Jessie and Stella somewhat. It helped Jessie to see that her thoughts and feelings were taken as seriously as those of her mother. Communication modeling and coaching were also important. The psychiatrist consistently spoke in a calm and validating manner. He would remind Stella to not react to Jessie's degrading comments. When Jessie began screaming a steady stream of obscenities and accusations in her phone calls to me, I would tell her we needed to end the call and give her permission to call me later when she had cooled down. This increased her anger in the moment, but empowered her to assertively communicate her frustrations, feelings, and needs.

Anyone meeting Jessie today would have difficulty imagining the bleak circumstances of her life only a few years ago. Jessie is one of the most remarkable young clients I have worked with in my nine-year social work career at this county Human Services Department. She completed her senior year credits over the summer and will graduate in June with her high school classmates.

During her junior year, Jessie maintained a 4.0 grade point average and was inducted into the National Honor Society. Currently, she is enrolled in two college-level courses at an area vocational school. Nothing seems to be out of reach for Jessie in this seventeenth year of her life. She is bright, articulate, and compassionate and has learned to use these personal attributes to advocate for herself and for others. Jessie continues to experience periodic manic episodes. During these times she still makes decisions that she later regrets. The most significant change is that Jessie is now able to reach out and contact people in her support network. This network no longer consists of only Human Services workers. It includes her family, friends in her peer groups, and the guidance counselors and educators she has worked with over the past year. Janie has dropped the role of family guardian. She has established an identity of her own, excels in school and engages in typical forms of sibling rivalry and rebelliousness in the home. Stella has become an adept advocate for herself and her children. She calls me from time to time to say, "You would have been so proud of me today." Then she describes how she advocated for her rights, and always adds a final—"And I never called him an asshole once—even though he acts like one."

Questions for Students

Summarize the difficulties displayed by Jessie, her sister (Janie), and their mother (Stella). Identify the empowerment strategies that were used to intervene with Jessie, with Janie, and with Stella. Assume you were the social worker for Jessie and the other members of this family. What would you have done differently to improve services to this family? Jessie was diagnosed as having a variety of disorders: substance addiction, conduct disorder, bipolar disorder with psychotic features, intermittent explosive disorder, antisocial personality disorder, posttraumatic stress disorder, and borderline personality disorder. What are the benefits of labeling someone with a mental disorder? What are the negative consequences of being labeled with a mental disorder? Assume you are Jessie—as a young girl/woman, how would you view yourself if you were labeled with these multiple disorders?

Chapter 6: Family Problems and Services to Families

Counseling A Woman Who is a Victim of Domestic Abuse
Krista Rasmussen

Credentials:

MSW, December 2002
BSW, December 2000

I am currently completing my final graduate field placement as a domestic violence counselor at a shelter for battered and abused women. The mission of the agency is to provide safety and support for women and their families and to facilitate their development. All the services at this facility are free and include: emergency shelter, transitional living, legal advocacy, counseling, employment, community education, and childcare services.

Case Example:

After Samantha Matson, 32, finished filling out our agency's paperwork, I asked her what she would like to talk about. She began by asking me to look at her. I looked at Samantha. I saw a petite young woman probably in her early thirties, who had straight, shoulder length blond hair. Her eyes, well I couldn't quite tell what their color was because they were swollen and black and blue. Though I did notice Samantha had a cast on her wrist and lower forearm, this was not all I saw. After looking at Samantha she then asked me to tell her what I saw. I told her I saw a young woman sitting across from me who is obviously very brave and has a tremendous amount of strength for seeking out our services. Samantha replied by saying that she obviously does not have a lot of strength because she was unable to prevent her injuries. I asked her, if she felt comfortable enough, to tell me about the injuries. Samantha did not hesitate at all to begin to tell me her story:

Samantha stated that her husband, Joe, and she have been married for four years. They have a 3-year-old daughter, Susie, and Samantha has a son, Adam, 9 years old, and a daughter, Katie, 7 years old from previous relationships. The first few months of her marriage with Joe, everything was wonderful. However, after the birth of Susie, Samantha and her two older children saw a side of Joe they had never witnessed before. Joe started to neglect Samantha's older children and would become irate with Samantha when she was attentive to them. Joe began to physically abuse both Samantha and her son. The Department of Human Services became involved with their family after the social worker at Adam's school questioned him about his bruises. Samantha stated that she and Joe were mandated to attend parenting classes and Joe was mandated to attend an anger management class. For approximately a year after attending the classes things were actually going well for the family. Samantha said she enjoyed this time when things were going well, but she was always on the edge, worried that something violent may happen again. Her worst nightmare came to fruition approximately a week before she came in for services. Joe beat her in front of their children.

Strategies used with the client:

After listening to Samantha's story, I thanked her for sharing part of her life with me. Her first question was, "So, should I leave him, or should I stay?" I let Samantha know that her question about whether or not she should stay or leave her husband is very common among the clients we see. I told her it would be very easy for me to make the decision for her, but this is not my job and she is the ultimate decision-maker. I explained my role and boundaries as a counselor, and let Samantha know that I was here to listen to her, assess her safety, support her, educate her, guide her, and help her set her own goals and make her own decisions, but I was not here to give her all the answers. Samantha appeared to be a bit confused by my response and stated she thought the counselor was supposed to tell his or her clients what to do. I again reviewed my role as a counselor and conveyed that I had confidence in her to make her own decisions.

I explained to Samantha that a crucial role of our agency is to educate our clientele on the issues surrounding domestic violence. I discussed with her the cycle of domestic violence and together we articulated a safety plan in case a violent event was to occur again.

Toward the end of our first session I informed Samantha about other services offered at this facility and in the community. I let her know that if she wanted additional information about the available services she could take a folder containing informational brochures that describe them in depth.

At the conclusion of this session I asked Samantha if she would like to continue seeing me for individual sessions and if she would like to, how often she would like to come in. Samantha decided to continue coming in once a week. Again, I complimented Samantha for seeking our services. As Samantha was leaving, she took an informational packet.

One week later we met again. I began the session by asking Samantha about her goals. Her main goal was to be able to make the decision about whether or not to leave her husband. I then asked Samantha the important question of what would help her make that decision. She answered that she would need to know if she could ever be able to live on her own with her children.

During the next four weeks, Samantha and I met individually on a regular basis; Samantha also attended the domestic violence support group and brought her children in weekly to meet with a counselor.

During our individual sessions, we explored what Samantha felt she needed in order to live on her own. I listened intently to her ideas and gave her feedback upon request. At the end of each session I verbally reviewed what Samantha talked about and highlighted all of her accomplishments. Even if she had taken a step back instead of forward, I complimented her for trying and let her know I still had confidence in her. I also commended Samantha for attending the support group and bringing her children in for counseling.

Outcome:

At the beginning of our sixth session, Samantha let me know that she was ready to make the decision about whether or not to leave her husband. Before even asking what her decision was, I inquired about what helped her feel prepared to make the decision. She replied that for one of the first times in her life she felt supported. She said it was extremely helpful for her to come and talk with someone who truly listened, cared, and believed what she had to say. She felt secure in making the decision because she was informed of the available community resources, many of which she was able to access. She also mentioned it was beneficial being educated on domestic violence. Finally, Samantha stated what was most helpful was that throughout the duration of our sessions, she came to the realization that she did not deserve to be abused and actually had the right to make the decision.

Summary:
Domestic violence is about power and control. It is imperative when working with clients such as Samantha to allow and encourage them to be in control and have power over what happens during the counseling sessions. Practicing this skill in a safe environment helps them to apply this to other areas of their lives. Throughout all our counseling sessions I never once told Samantha what she needed to do. I was simply there to listen, support, guide, and educate her. In the end Samantha was able to meet her goal and make the decision. There were times during our sessions that Samantha thanked me for what I had done for her, though I always reminded her that she was the one doing all the work.

Questions for Students:

Identify the strengths perspectives and empowerment strategies that this field intern used with this client. The husband, Joe, was sometimes a good husband and father, and at other times he was very abusive to his wife, Samantha. What are the likely reasons why Joe sometimes became abusive? What services might have been provided to him that would have been more effective in curbing the abuse? It took a long time for Samantha to decide to leave her abusive husband. Why do you think a number of women stay in abusive relationships for a long time? If you were the social worker for Samantha, how would you have proceeded differently?

Chapter 7: Sexual Orientation and Services to GLBT Individuals

Group Therapy with Non-Offending Parents of Sexually Abused Children
Deborah L. Cornella, MSW, CISW

Credentials:

MSW, CISW (Certified Independent Social Worker)

Currently I am a group therapist at an agency that provides a variety of treatment services to sexually abused children and to nonoffending parents of sexually abused children; these services include a 24-hour support telephone service, therapy groups, support groups, and parental educational workshops for children and parents when abuse has occurred.). As a group therapist at this facility, I facilitate groups for both sexually abused children, and also groups for non-offending parents of sexually abused children.

Prior experience includes fifteen years of social work practice as an ongoing case worker, child sexual abuse investigation, and elementary school social work.

Case Example:

Having to deal with the sexual abuse of their child can be overwhelming and devastating for non-offending parents. The gamut of emotions parents feel include: isolation, anger, embarrassment, guilt, and self-blame. Trust has often been violated by a significant person in their lives. They feel they no longer have control of their child's life or their own, and question if they will be able to trust anyone again. Parents join therapy groups hoping to help their child, and to find ways to deal with the pain. They also want to have the support of others that are facing this problem.

Empowerment of individuals through the group process takes place when members begin to feel they are regaining better control of their lives. In the group setting they find a safe place, where they can talk about the abuse. The group therapist needs to respect group members, and treat them with dignity, while providing genuine support and direction. However, allowing the members to share control of their group is a first step towards their healing and empowerment. Basic group rules are agreed upon in the first group meeting. These rules establish safety, boundaries, and respect. The dynamics of the group process connect parents to each other, which motivates them to take positive action towards improving their circumstances. This builds the foundation for members to start to trust again, through their relationships with group members. Each group member needs to have time to vent their pain and address their own issues. Through disclosure, discussion and receiving affirmation from each other, members gain strength. When members are able to give support and insight to each other, they have internalized concepts, and can feel they are making a difference through sharing their feedback. This can be a positive and powerful experience for them.

Self-care, time with their child, educational information about sexual abuse, parenting methods, and ways to deal with stress are focuses during group. The concept of self-care is hard for some parents to accept, as this idea may seem selfish to them. Gradually they realize they need to meet some of their own needs in order to have the energy to give to their child. Children who make the most progress in their own therapy, are those who are believed and supported by their non-offending parents. Group therapy enables a parent to provide support to their child because they are feeling supported themselves. Through the dynamics of the group process, members feel energy and are eager to come back and share their progress with each other. Members are encouraged to journal on their own. This is an active way to deal with pain and to facilitate the discovery of the emotions that underlie their thoughts and actions, which can influence change. Educational concepts are presented on parenting and aspects of sexual abuse. Written handouts reinforce this information. Ending each session with deep breathing and relaxation exercises helps parents deal with stress and transition from the work of the group back to their daily lives.

One of the group members, Jen, has a ten-year-old daughter who was sexually maltreated by her teenage stepbrother. Jen discovered the abuse and felt tremendous guilt and self-blame, since she was present in the home during the incidents of abuse. Jen was timid, quiet, and soft-spoken, and shared little about herself or her situation for several group meetings. She was under incredible stress because her husband and his relatives blamed her for the maltreater no longer being able to reside in the home. Her daughter was clinging to her and Jen felt uncertain if she wished to remain in her marriage.

Jen has progressed to becoming a leader in the group. Now she smiles often, has a positive outlook, is handling her anger, is more relaxed, and is dealing with the stress. She motivated the group by encouraging them to take care of themselves. She became more involved with her children and consistent in her parenting. She feels the group has become an "extended family" for her. She feels safe in group, and has openly shared more during each meeting. She has internalized many of the concepts learned in group, which enables her to be supportive towards other members. Attending group was a step that took a lot of courage for her. During group she talked about wanting to attend college in a nursing program and the group enthusiastically supported this idea. Due to this encouragement, Jen did start school and her self-confidence continues to grow. She has protected her daughter by not allowing any contact with her stepson, although this has negatively affected her marriage. She has given her husband the choice to participate in marriage counseling, or to end the marriage. Jen and her daughter are continuing to deal with the aftermath of the abuse. She now speaks openly with the group, and feels she receives and gives support and encouragement there.

Each of the group members has progressed in some of the same ways as Jen, as well as in other areas. The members have become a cohesive group, and are respectful and caring towards each other. They share their tears, and now they share their daughter. After several sessions, this group is so cohesive it is capable of functioning independently. They have grown to the point where contribution by the therapist is minimal. Members enjoy each other, and through the bond of their group dynamics they share their progress and accomplishments each week, and they also find the empathy and acceptance that they need.

When the group terminates, they will take with them the knowledge that they and their child will continue to deal with the pain of abuse throughout their lives, yet they also feel they can cope better with the skills they have acquired in group. They have begun to trust again, through the relationships they have built with group members. They have accomplished many of their goals, and have hope for their children and themselves.

Questions for Students:

Identify the empowerment strategies that this therapist used with this group, and with the client (Jen). If you were the parent of a daughter who has been sexually abused, how would you feel? What services would you need to handle your negative feelings? How do you think a ten-year-old girl would feel if she was sexually maltreated by her teenage stepbrother? What services would she need to cope with this traumatic experience? What might the social worker do differently to improve services to non-offending parents?

Chapter 7: Sexual Orientation, Sexual Concerns, and Sex Counseling

Empowering a Young Male to Confront his Sexual Curiosity and to Terminate his Sexual Misconduct
Mark R. Young, MSSW, ACSW

Credentials:

    Academic:
      B.A. Social Work, 1986
      MSSW, 1988

Case Example:

    Immediately after completing graduate school, overly anxious about finding a job, I jumped (North, five hours) at the first opportunity that came along. It was a clinical social work/psychotherapist position for an outpatient mental health center in the Midwest. My caseload consisted of roughly half kids, half adults, and ten to fifteen percent were court-ordered to attend for various reasons.

    One day I had a young adolescent male attend his intake appointment, referred by the probate court to address his recent sexual misconduct charges. I'll refer to him as "Artie." Like most sexual offenders I've worked with, Artie initially downplayed his actions, telling me he really "didn't do anything wrong." He was "just playing" with a younger neighbor boy; he explained that his friend's mom "just wants to get me in trouble." Fortunately, I got in the habit of asking for a police incident report. The immature, 13-year-old squirmed as I tried to sensitively read through the contents of the incident report. The younger boy, approximately 10, alleged that he and Artie took off their clothes, touched each other, and that Artie eventually "put his dingy in my butt." It was the opinion of the court that partial penetration may have occurred.

    Squirming more, embarrassed, and slightly stuttering in an inflected, crackling voice, Artie insisted the report was "*not true!* I-I-I'm not *like* that!" I didn't try to dispute the report or his sexual orientation with him. You never know what to believe when your client swears to one scenario, and police or social services reports declare something sharply different. The accused sexual offenders I've worked with usually minimize the extent to which they are guilty of their charges—especially before they've been adjudicated and sentenced. My philosophy is that it is better to risk being gullible when in doubt, than to be cynical and wrongly accuse someone, or call them a liar without proof. Once a first-time "perpetrator" has been sentenced (often to counseling and community service), it is much easier to get them to open up. After all, they are *already* having to pay the penalty for being guilty and they have little to lose by being open at that point.

In the weeks and months that followed, our rapport grew. I was able to get Artie to believe that I genuinely liked him, that he could trust me to keep our conversations private and confidential, but that I believed at least *some* of the incident report was accurate. Further, I explained that I still would accept him regardless of what happened that day. He grew up in the country—a pretty sheltered life. He felt the need to convince me that he wasn't homosexual, even blaming his younger friend, the victim, for the event. I talked to him about the oft-quoted statistic that at least "10%" of the population is believed to be exclusively homosexual. Amidst his many nervous interruptions, attesting that "I'm not one of them", I assured him that it wouldn't matter; that I didn't care either way, and that I wouldn't think any differently of him if he were. I explained to him that he would be in the same trouble if the younger child friend had been a girl. Eventually he realized that I would continue to accept him, regardless of what happened that day. I believe he was sexually curious, intrigued about puberty and bodily sensations, and his younger playmate was a willing, vulnerable subject for his exploration.

He gradually admitted, or "remembered" doing essentially all the significant behaviors outlined in the reports we had discussed before. He found it much easier to admit and talk about events as "experimentation," though we did address the fact that *he* was the older child, who was being trusted and looked up to. We also discussed the potential physical and psychological damage that may have occurred. I believe the pleasure he derived from the sexual behaviors caused conflict for him. His male peers at the country school were not very accepting of homosexuality. I tried to help him understand that both males and females can experience pleasurable, sensual touch from other males, females, or themselves. Furthermore, a male experiencing such pleasurable touch from another male no more proves homosexuality than pleasurable touch from a female proves or determines that he is "straight."

I don't recall all the details of our work, but I believe he stayed somewhat friends with that other boy, and didn't re-offend. He returned to see me voluntarily once about seven years ago, during a family crisis, and again in the past year. He has been married twice, having chosen a heterosexual lifestyle, which he seems very content with. He still feels my office is a safe place to come when he can't handle the situations in his life.

In retrospect, I realize my methods with Artie followed Jack Annon's PLISSIT Model of intervention*. Annon suggested this concept in sexual therapy work. It was consistent with the increasing push around that time in all forms of education and treatments for the *least restrictive environment*. I had to memorize the PLISSIT model for an exam in my BSW methods course work. It suggests approaching interventions and change efforts with clients with progressively more involved efforts, giving:

Permission, **L**imited **I**nformation, **S**pecific **S**uggestions, and if necessary, **I**ntensive **T**herapy. (A summary of this PLISSIT model is provided in the Zastrow text.)

I suspect he still has his share of crises from one day to the next, but he hasn't had any sexual misconduct charges against him for over ten years.

* Annon, J. "The PLISSIT model: a proposed conceptual scheme for behavioral treatment of sexual problems", *Journal of Sex Education Therapy*. 1976.

Questions for Students:

Describe the PLISSIT model. In what ways is this model consistent with empowerment? Identify the specific ways in which the social worker empowered Artie to confront his sexual curiosity and to terminate his sexual misconduct. How did the social worker display a nonjudgmental attitude towards gay men? Would you classify Artie as being "gay" for his sexual involvement with another male? Why, or why not? What is your definition of being a gay man/lesbian? Do you think it is desirable to use psychotherapy to seek to change the sexual orientation of someone who is gay (or lesbian) to a heterosexual orientation? Why, or why not? If you were the social worker for Artie, what would you have done differently?

Chapter 8: Drug Abuse and Drug Treatment Programs

Motivational Enhanced Therapy for a Person with a Drug Addiction
Dianne Bowker, MS, APSW

Credentials:

BA, Social Work
MS, Guidance and Counseling
APSW (Advanced Practice Social Worker)
Agency: A Department of Corrections/Division of Community Corrections Agency

Case Example:

"Why do you want him on your caseload?"
"You're asking for trouble!"
"In his family the hospital might as well assign a Department of Corrections number along with the birth certificate."

Those were some of the milder comments I received when I requested that Arturo Hernandez be transferred to me for supervision. Back then I had no idea what I would put into, and get out of, this case.

I met Arturo when he had been placed on supervision for multiple counts of Manufacture/Delivery of a Controlled Substance. His prior agent had ordered that he attend a group I was facilitating as part of my Probation/Parole Agent duties. He had long sparkling black hair and an engaging smile. He wore the gold jewelry of a drug dealer and drove a well cared for Camaro. Appearance alone would have made him stand out in the small town probation/parole office. Arturo however, was much more than appearance.

Everyone in Social Services has a favorite type of client. I like the bright ones, a little older, the ones who have been around the system for a while and honed their own survival techniques—no matter how maladaptive those techniques might be. I call them the flyers. Intelligent and charismatic, they have so many gifts that if they would address their problems they could "fly." Arturo fit this description to a T. He never finished high school but his intelligence was obvious. The other members of the group hung on his words when he spoke. He had no hesitation speaking about what was going on in his life. He had the rare ability to speak to a group and yet seem to be addressing each individual member. Within a matter of weeks he became the acknowledged leader. Shortly thereafter he was revoked and sent to prison. This case example is about what went wrong and what went right in the case plan of Arturo.

What went wrong is easy. Mr. Hernandez continued to deal cocaine for several more months until he was arrested. Why it went wrong is hard to explain because there is no one problem. Arturo hated the correctional system. He was not about to "be saved" just because his agent demanded that he not use drugs. To be able to control his direction in life was important to him and he had no plans to give that control to an assigned agent. He refrained from drug use but got a psychological high from being "the man," the one who had cocaine in his pocket. Arturo was close to his family ... too close. His brothers and other family members were on supervision or in prison for the same type of behavior. Using drugs and dealing drugs was "normal" within his family system. Lastly, and perhaps most importantly, Arturo could not picture himself in another lifestyle. There is a high probability that if you can't see a goal you will never obtain it.

What went right was using Motivational Enhanced Therapy (MET) as a form of intervention. It is easy to look at this individual and say he needs drug treatment. For social workers, especially those with the immense power of probation/parole agents, it is easy to get lost in all the programs that the client must do so that they will "get better." What we forget to do is to listen and to give assertions of positive attributes. MET is based on listening and gentle confrontation. It uses suggestions instead of demands and gives the client a choice about treatment or other issues that will affect his or her life. It also uses positive assertions as feedback.

Mr. Hernandez was already facing revocation when he was officially placed on my caseload. However, I was fortunate in that I had the opportunity to meet him in my group and to have been able to tell him some of the things I believed were possible for him. I believe this is one of the most important things I do as a social worker. I acknowledge people's strengths and give them a view of themselves as a connected, stable member of the community. Many of the people I see have never been told what is positive about them. Secondly, I offer choices. I work very hard to refrain from the "my way or the highway" approach. I prefer to give a number of possibilities that the offender can choose from to help him or her make the desired changes. The person I must work on when I am engaged in this type of treatment is not the offender, but myself. How many possible routes to new behavior are available? What are the positive attributes of that person? Am I hearing what the person says and willing to react to that and not hearing only what I want to hear? Do I have the information available that the individual needs to hear and can I present it in an educated, professional manner?

Arturo Hernandez is now a success story. He no longer uses, or sells drugs. He has taken control of his life and is a positive member of the community. He works in the addiction field and has an exceptional rapport with correctional clients. Currently he is working to return to school to earn his Bachelor's degree in Social Work. I have asked him many times what made the difference for him and his reply has always been "someone who cared enough about me to hear what I had to say and the positive assertions."

I have emphasized <u>listening</u> in writing this case example. It seems only fair to listen to Arturo and see if his statement concurs with what I believe I saw happen.

Arturo: "When I first heard from my PO the night I got arrested she said, 'Do you know that someday you're going to be somebody?' I thought to myself, 'Yeah, right. You're f------ crazy lady!' Little did I know that those words would help me to get to where I am today—an AODA counselor with an Associates degree in alcohol and other drug treatment. What I know now is that because someone believed in me, believed that someday I could be someone, I made great many changes. I just wasn't ready to hear about that possibility back then.

Regardless of what I was doing—criminal behavior, using cocaine, selling cocaine—this person always believed in me. I was the one who needed to make the decision to change. She believed in me even when I got arrested. She believed I could still turn things around. She came to visit me in the county jail where I was waiting to get revoked and sent to prison. She asked me to stop and think about what was coming my way (prison) and to make the prison work for me. For the first time I heard what was being said to me, although by now I had placed my future in the hands of the

Department of Corrections. I went to prison ready for change because of the intervention used by my probation officer in an old county jail. I went to prison looking for the positive out of whatever would happen to me.

The whole time I was in prison, 2 years, 9 months, she wrote me once a month. She never gave me answers. She made me go out and seek what I wanted, the changes that would give me a positive lifestyle. She pointed me in the right direction but emphasized that I would have to find the path that was best for me to use to get to my destination.

Four years after our meeting in the jail, while attending school, I learned the modality she used on me—MET. When I read the information on Motivational Enhanced Therapy I realized how my probation officer had let me show myself that I had the power to change me, but not until I was ready. The decision for change was mine to make and mine alone. As an AODA counselor I use MET combined with Reality Based Therapy in my work with clients. I believe they need to hear that they have the power to change. Even though life gets difficult at times, it is okay. Okay—you can succeed.

I owe my probation officer my life. She helped me find out what was really important to me and how my behavior was affecting me getting those things I wanted."

Questions for Students:

How is Motivational Enhanced Therapy consistent with the strengths perspective and the empowerment approach? What limitations do you see with MET? For example, do you think the approach will work with severely depressed individuals, or with patients who have Alzheimer's Disease? If you were the probation/parole agent for Arturo, what would you have done differently to improve services to him? Do you believe it is likely that Arturo will again return to using or selling drugs? Why, or why not? What are reasons why it is so difficult for someone who has used extensively (and sold) drugs in the past to refrain from doing so in the future?

Chapter 9: Crime, Juvenile Delinquency, and Correctional Services

Parole Services for an Individual with Multiple Criminal Convictions
Dianne Bowker, MS, APSW

Credentials:

BA, Social Work
MS, Guidance and Counseling
APSW (Advanced Practice Social Worker)
Agency: A Department of Corrections/Division of Community Corrections Agency

Case Example:

When you're assigned a file in the Department of Corrections, you always hope it's not a big one. The file I was given made the legs of my metal desk creak, not a good sign for the future. In it were yellowed newspaper clippings, years of smudged prison forms and inches of psychological assessments. The Pre-Sentence Investigation (a document given to the court that contains a social history and a recommendation for sentencing) portrayed one of the worst cases of child abuse I had the misfortune to read.

When Ryan Benson was two years old his mother remarried. His stepfather beat him with 2x4's when he did not eat his food fast enough or when he did not finish what was put on his plate. He was tied with ropes and locked in closets. When Ryan turned five he was not allowed in the house during the day. If he wet his pants he was made to wear those clothes unwashed the next day. Covered with bruises, dried urine and feces, Ryan was put outside and told to behave himself. School was another torment. He was placed in the "slow" class and labeled as antisocial when he did not play with the other children. By this time Ryan recoiled if anyone came too close to him or tried to touch him.

Eventually, relatives who believed he would soon be killed, talked his mother into allowing them to adopt him. The short, skinny child was moved from a deteriorated inner city neighborhood to a middle class suburb. He was given tutors to help him catch up with his schoolwork. He joined cub scouts and had his own body building equipment. It sounds like a happy ending—It wasn't.

One snowy winter evening his family went out to dinner with the next-door neighbors. Ryan, now a teenager, walked over to talk to that neighbor's daughter, a friend who attended the same high school. They drank some Coke and watched television. They snacked on some pizza. The girl told Ryan to leave because their parents would soon be getting home. Ryan did something entirely different. He picked up a knife and stabbed her over fifty times. Knife in hand, he walked home leaving a trail of blood in the sparkling snow. He climbed into bed without changing his bloody clothes and went to sleep. Police found him there within the hour.

The girl's family was well known in the community. The press had a heyday. Ryan answered any question he was asked, except for questions about the night of the murder. The court showed some leniency. Ryan was sentenced to 25 years of prison. His survivor instinct intact, he learned many things in prison, some good and some bad. He became the prison Brewmeister when he found out that drinking would take away some of the pain. He discovered drugs. He found out he was not "slow," but had an exceptionally high I.Q. He found the prison library where he devoured books on philosophy, religion, history, and metaphysics. He was initiated into the Indian Sweat Lodge. He still stayed to himself. He still didn't want anyone to touch him and he still refused to talk about "that" night.

When Ryan had done a little over 15 years of his time, he was paroled. The family that adopted him had stayed in touch but did not want him to return to their neighborhood. So he returned to the first neighborhood in the inner city to live with his aunt. He entered college and his grades were fine. He entered the drug trade and didn't do so well. He was charged in Federal Court and was placed on Federal Probation. He was revoked on his state charge and returned to prison for three more years. During those three years he again found himself a home in the library, but Ryan still didn't like being touched and he still wouldn't talk about "that" night.

When Ryan was paroled the second time, the family was no longer interested in having anything to do with him. He eventually found a job working for a small construction company in a local community. That's when the file was placed with a thud on my desk.

I still remember the first time I saw him. I had expected to see a large, bull-like man. The file said he spent as much time as possible working out in the gym. When I called his name a short, acne-scarred man in worn blue jeans came to the front. Soft-spoken, he introduced himself and followed me to my office. Somewhere in that 50-foot hallway I decided everything had been tried and I would just listen and affirm. Oh, he was under parole and would have to follow the rules, but I decided not to use the approach of "don't do this, and do that." I also did not want to make any attempt to force him to talk about the murder. If he had time, so did I. He couldn't decide he didn't want to see me any more—if he failed to show up he knew that I would issue a warrant for his arrest. It was with this decision that Ryan and I began the sharing of an odyssey.

At first we just talked about day-to-day things—what he was doing on the job, how well he liked his coworkers, and so on. But it soon became apparent that he was hungry for someone with whom he could talk philosophical ideologies and discuss religious concepts. Our conversations started to include spirituality and the monolithic Godhead. If anyone had listened in on our conversations they would have been surprised to discover us debating the existence of the unicorn outside of fairytales. It was not hard to find affirmations for Ryan. He was polite, had a great sense of humor, and a sharp mind. He not only spoke of respect often but also "practiced what he preached." For example, he would never touch another's possessions without first asking. He would never touch a metaphysical item, as that would show disrespect for the owner's beliefs. He would not become involved in a relationship with a woman because he was not capable of upholding his end of the relationship. Slowly, very slowly, our discussions started to focus more on Ryan's inner life. What did he remember of his childhood? What was it like being a sixteen-year-old thrown into the adult prison system? How did it feel being abandoned by his adopted family? I never displayed shock. I never said "wrong choice." I listened and affirmed whenever possible.

In the middle of the night one snowy winter, I received a call from police. Ryan was in a local hospital located about 50 miles away. He had been drinking and was found mugged. He wouldn't let the hospital take a blood test for alcohol. They let me talk to him over the phone. He agreed to the blood test. I told him I would talk to him in jail the next day. It was one of the few times that I had a hard time going to sleep after a police call in the middle of the night.

The next day it was difficult for me to make the call to the jail. I was angry. I had spent hours of time with this man and he broke one of the most basic rules of his parole—no drinking or drugs. He asked if he would have to go to jail in the county where I worked as an agent. My answer was yes. I asked him how good was his word and he couldn't answer so I revised the question. I asked how good was his word to me. His answer was, "pretty good." I did something I don't usually do. I released him on his word, knowing he was going to be put back in jail, to drive to the office. He drove to my office over snow-covered, icy roads. It was now I would see if my listening and affirmations would work. The questions were simple. Why did you go there? What were you doing? The answers were a surprise. Ryan had gone to the city to buy sex. Puda is the prison term. Now Ryan started to talk. He talked about the feeling of being disconnected. He talked about the loneliness and the fear that God could not forgive him. He explained that it was not the act of sex he was looking for, sexual acts did not lead him to feel connected for long periods of time, but they did give him a feeling of connection with another human being. He said that for a few minutes it helped. The emotions in the office were so intense that finally I put on my coat and we walked in the frigid winter air—Ryan talking and me listening. Finally, we ended up at the jail and I walked back to the office alone, but I couldn't get out of my mind one of the comments he made while walking; a comment about every soul being a star. Somehow, in Ryan's mind, he had destroyed a star. The power and shame behind that statement were overwhelming.

I didn't see him for months after that. The federal probation officer and I had placed him in inpatient treatment. After his treatment ended, he reported to my office. We talked about the treatment and his plans for the future. When he got up to leave, he had his hands clasped behind his back and I teased him that I wasn't going to put handcuffs on him. I laughed when I told him he could put his hands down. His answer amazes me to this day. The man who would not be touched said, "I keep them this way because I want to hug you." I turned around and gave him a hug. He hugged me back.

Note: All social workers have some defining moments. But we are not made to live in a constant emotional high. I don't want to leave you with the thought that everything was now fine. Ryan did start to talk. He even started to speak of "that" night. He promised I would hear it all. However, I never got to the end of the story. The night call this time was of death in an automobile accident—no alcohol or drugs indicated. I went outside in my robe and slippers and looked at the clear night sky—looking for a new star. It was a tribute, a sign of respect to a man who saw every soul a star.

Questions for Students:

This case example illustrates that (what is typical in perhaps most cases) full resolution of problems and issues of clients is not achieved. Identify, as specifically as possible, what evidence is there that Ryan Benson was making progress in ending his criminal behavior and ending his use of illegal drugs. Also, what evidence is there that Ryan was making progress in resolving his emotional difficulties? Identify the strategies that this probation and parole officer used in assisting Mr. Benson to make progress in these areas. If you were the probation and parole officer for Ryan Benson, what would you have done differently to improve services to him? What services would have been beneficial to this probation and parole officer after she was informed Ryan had been killed in an automobile accident? This probation and parole officer hugged Mr. Benson at one point. Do you believe this hug was appropriate? When is it appropriate, and inappropriate, to hug a client?

Chapter 10: Problems in Education and School Social Work

Support Groups at School for Young Girls Who are Living in Families with Spousal Abuse
Donald Nolan, MSSW, BCD

Credentials:

Donald Nolan is a school social worker in a public school system.

Case Example:

The difficulties that children face have changed enormously in the past 20-30 years. Schools have adjusted to societal and family difficulties and have developed programs to assist children so that they can better learn at school. An increasingly difficult dilemma facing children, especially girls, is the issue of spousal abuse. Although there are individual differences, most abuse, physical and/or emotional, is directed from a male (father) to a female (mother). This creates a confusing situation for girls no matter their age. They do not understand why this is happening, what has caused it, who is to "blame," and perhaps most importantly, why it continues. Mothers in this situation often develop a victim mentality. They do not perceive that they have options and/or that they can control their lives. Certainly they do not feel empowered. Thus, children in this type of family situation may come to school worried about their mothers, and feeling that their world is not very predictable.

It is in this scenario that student assistance groups can be vehicles for change. In our school system one of the responsibilities of school social workers is to be group facilitators for support groups for such girls. The girls are usually referred by the teachers. Each Student Assistance Group has several girls in it, and is facilitated by one or two social workers. Groups meet once a week for 45 minutes, for 8 to 10 weeks.

We do not want these children to perceive themselves as victims. They need to better understand the dynamics of the family situation, and that they are not alone—other children have to deal with similar situations. More importantly, they need to understand that they have not created any difficulties in the family that could have caused one parent to abuse another. Far too often abusers verbally blame anyone but themselves for their actions. Thus, if a wife, domestic partner, or girlfriend does not make sure that there are no problems in the home, they sometimes erroneously conclude they deserve to be punished when family problems arise. In a verbal exchange in this type of situation, a child might hear "why aren't you taking care of Jenny's behavior at school" or "why can't the kids pick up around here, this place is a mess."

Children also need to understand they cannot control the behavior of a parent. They cannot behave perfectly. They cannot stop their father or mother's boyfriend from doing anything. They do not have the physical or emotional ability to do anything about it. The reality is that they need to protect themselves in these situations without feeling guilty about not "helping" their mothers.

What a dilemma they are in. It is easy to see how girls in this situation can feel powerless, guilty, and vulnerable. Such girls can benefit significantly from a support group. They need to develop some ability to distance themselves from this spousal abuse. They need to identify with women who behave in more independent and powerful ways. Discussions about role models such as independent women teachers, or women in the community or in the state or national public scene help girls to become empowered to see that there are alternatives in their lives. Frank discussions about not letting this happen to them are also helpful. Girls can encourage each other to be strong and fight back even if this is not possible for their mother. Then there is the issue of women feeling the strength to leave a bad situation. To do this, individuals need confidence in themselves, and financial opportunities. What better way to do this than by doing well in school academics so that one has possibilities for post secondary education? Career possibilities need to be discussed and girls need to develop goals for their financial future.

It all seems like a lot to do in one 45-minute, weekly meeting for 8-10 weeks. Yet, much is accomplished in this time period. Girls, even in elementary school, can be empowered to look at life differently. They can develop more confidence in their academic potential. They can develop goals for careers that leave them less dependent on others. They can learn they are not alone and that openly talking with others can help to clarify that there often are constructive options in life. They can learn to understand, but not accept, the plight of their mother. They can learn that they can help each other, if not their mothers, to be strong, independent, and capable.

Jenny is an example of one such young woman. A 5th grade student, she came to school one day clearly upset. Her grades had dropped during the year and her teacher had been sensing that Jenny was not as focused on school as she had been earlier in the year. In a conversation with the school social worker that morning, this bright but troubled youngster talked about the spousal abuse at home last night. She was confused and worried about her mother, and angry at her father who had abused her mother. The anger was a constructive emotion for her and one that could help her connect with the ideas of empowerment. She joined a group of other girls and quickly became an excellent addition. Her focus returned to school academics and she started getting even better grades. The spousal abuse in her family did not change much during the rest of that year. But, Jenny smiled more, got acknowledgement for her grades from others, and started talking about wanting to be a teacher. She again was thriving, as she improved her self-concept and her self-confidence.

Questions for Students:

Summarize the specific empowering objectives that school social workers seek to attain in facilitating support groups for girls living in families where spousal abuse is occurring. Also summarize what these social workers do to achieve these objectives. Emotionally and behaviorally, how are young girls apt to be affected by growing up in families where there are frequent episodes of spousal abuse? How are boys apt to be affected differently than girls when raised in families where the father occasionally abuses the mother? What services are needed for the mother and the father in families where the father occasionally abuses the mother? If you were a school social worker providing services to young girls being raised in families where there is spousal abuse, what would you do differently than what the school social workers are doing in this case example?

Chapter 11: Work-Related Problems and Social Work in the Workplace

Improving Morale in an Organization
Mark R. Young, MSSW, ACSW

Credentials:

Academic:
B.A. Social Work, 1986
MSSW, 1988

Case Example:

After moving to a small, rural community in the upper Midwest, I was initially busy learning my new job, setting up my apartment, and finding my way around. Eventually, I had some time on my hands, and started exploring ways to have fun in my new community, and I began playing in tennis and volleyball leagues. I met a great lifelong friend in the process. Blaise worked at the local hospital, and invited me to many outings, parties, and events. He was a real social organizer for lots of fun activities that many people participated in. Knowing him helped me get to know countless people in the community and quickly feel like I was at "home" in this new location. I also learned a few things about getting people together for fun recreation, which I took back to my own workplace, which was at a community mental health counseling center.

I was the new kid on the block at the agency, and eventually I noticed problems with morale. Workers felt unappreciated and felt that management wasn't concerned about their needs. Some management personnel had difficulty connecting with staff. Some workers resented each other. Most of us were very overwhelmed, unable to keep up with the growing wait list for services and increased paperwork requirements from the agency and state. There were interagency conflicts and also poor relations at times.

Staff meetings were often very uncomfortable scenarios. People were often quiet, keeping their concerns and gripes or hostilities inside. There was little eye contact. Therapists avoided volunteering to make case presentations—in my opinion we all were somewhat leery of "exposing" ourselves and our work; I think we chose not to be vulnerable in front of the group. When a supervisor or manager requested a volunteer, I was often the only one volunteering. Granted, I was probably more comfortable with public speaking than the others, but I think the low morale put a further kibosh on any "beyond the call of duty" activity.

Following my friend Blaise's examples, I organized a softball game between the local department of social services and our agency. I made sure to post the event in other departments, where the morale was probably better, to ensure a sufficient number signed up. I also conspired with a couple key people at the other agency, who were able to fill up a team to take us on.

The agency had summer picnics in the past, but I think they had fallen by the wayside prior to my joining the staff, so I again kicked into gear with help from others and organized an annual staff picnic, getting a great turnout with many potluck dishes. After this I started organizing "Comedy Night" outings to a local club and enthusiasm continued. I was told the agency used to have annual "all-staff" meetings, and I joined forces with others to organize the first one in several years. It gave various departments recognition, introduced all the staff to each other, and increased a sense of common identity. Other activities that I organized with help of others at the agency included: river tubing, whitewater rafting, Halloween/Costume parties, and a men's volleyball team. As new mandates for completion of multiple new forms came about, staff began feeling stressed. I was annoyed by how inefficiently the new forms were laid out, repetition of content, and waste of paper. I stayed late at work and revised many of them into a single facesheet, that was adopted and used for years. I also created forms that streamlined the tracking of paperwork requirements for other staff.

The group of about ten on-call crisis workers really disliked having to give up many weekends and weeknights to sit by the phone for a buck and a half an hour. Much complaining had been done for the past year or two, but no one really tried to make a formal request for any kind of change. Several told me "they don't care; it'll never change."

During much discussion at our "emergency/on-call meetings" Friday afternoons, and moments of venting to each other throughout the week, I started putting together a formal proposal with input from everyone. The "old timers" told me the rate hadn't changed since they started eight years prior. This was great ammo! I wrote this up nicely and we had it presented at the next board meeting. They unanimously agreed to raise the flat rate a dollar per hour, and *added* something called "field time," where we were paid time and a half if we got called out of our homes for a crisis intervention! Everyone was happy with this (and many people *asked* to take each other's on-call to make extra Christmas money, etc.)

My friend Pam had worked at another agency in Wisconsin where they had a tradition known as "P.O.E.T.'s CLUB (Piss On Everything, Tomorrow's Saturday)—sort of a TGIF idea, or "business after hours" for human service agency employees. She and I began a tradition at our agencies, and soon other agencies were taking their turns organizing the next month's POET's meeting. Occasionally, many years later, we still resurrect a POET's Club after-hours get-together.

I was asked to do the agency newsletter, after the previous editor left the agency, and agreed to keep this going. It gave recognition to those who needed it, and provided a great opportunity to poke some fun at each other and keep us from taking our jobs too seriously.

Since I left the mental health center several years ago, they have started other social/recreational events and traditions—grilling out/picnicking over the lunch hour every summer; wearing blue jeans on Fridays; and reading and discussing journal articles one Friday a month over lunch. Most of these events integrate different departments and support staff, and are probably great for morale.

Currently I work part-time at a hemodialysis center, and I organize annual staff-patient picnics each summer, and I occasionally produce a unit newsletter, featuring both patients and staff. I also continue to play in volleyball and tennis leagues—I've gotten pretty decent over the past 14 years! Getting involved with these different sport leagues and taking occasional night classes for fun (pottery, electronics and welding) has helped me to meet many dozens of friends, colleagues, and acquaintances since I relocated to this part of the country. It has helped me immeasurably to link clients with services and resources, to get referrals, and to have a positive impact on morale, to feel more connected to each other, and to have more than just a "working relationship." Many of us now have lifelong friendships with each other.

Aside from whatever good these pursuits may have had on the morale of staff, I think they also helped a young clinical social worker (me) stay busy, and compensate for those beleaguering waves of self-doubt and inadequacy that can plague a fresh-out-of-school social worker.

Questions for Students:

In addition to empowering an individual, group, family, or community, a social worker also needs at times to empower an organization. In this case example, the social worker sought to improve morale at the organization at which he was employed. Describe what this social worker specifically did to improve morale at this community mental health counseling center. When morale at an organization is improved, why are the staff apt to provide better services to clients? What other strategies might be used to improve morale at an organization where morale is low? What factors tend to improve morale at an organization? What factors tend to foster deterioration of morale at an organization? When is it desirable to employ a consultant on "team building" to improve morale?

Chapter 12: Racism, Ethnocentrism, and Strategies for Advancing Social and Economic Justice

Empowering A Hmong Client to Make Positive Changes
Philip P. Yang, M.S.

Credentials:

Master of Science Degree, May 2002
Emphasis: Guidance and Counseling in Higher Education

Bachelor of Arts, August 1998
Major: Social Work
Minor: Marketing

Case Example:

I did a field placement for my undergraduate degree with Joining Forces for Families (JFF). JFF is a unit within many county Human Services agencies. It serves a diverse spectrum of clients, including whites, African Americans, Asians, Hispanics, and others. The purpose of JFF is to assure that needy families with children who are eligible for public assistance have access to resources, such as food, shelter, clothing, medical care, counseling, education, and employment training.

The goal is helping these families become self-sufficient. My internship responsibilities focused on assisting low income families—making home visits, linking families to resources, providing transportation for clients, and interpreting Wisconsin Works (W-2) laws and regulations to Southeast Asian-American families who have limited English skills. (Wisconsin's Temporary Assistance to Needy Families Program is called Wisconsin Works).

Client's Problems:

I was assigned to make a home visit to a Hmong family in Wisconsin. A caseworker from the County Human Services agency referred Mr. Due's case to us, as Mr. Vue had not participated in Employment Training in the last three months—and therefore was suspended from receiving Food Stamps, W-2 benefits, and Medical Assistance. The referring agency asked us to investigate why Mr. Vue was no longer participating in Employment Training. As a young and inexperienced social work intern, I felt a little bit nervous about the case. However, I had the advantage of being fluent in both Hmong and English. As my supervisor, Heidi Boushon, and I entered their house, I could smell the special odors coming from their living room. I greeted the father by calling him Mr. Vue and we shook hands. Mr. Vue was about 48 years old, married, and had eight children (five sons and three daughters). The children's ages ranged from eight through seventeen years old. As I looked at the walls around the house, they seemed to be cracked and deteriorated. The children observed me quietly as I spoke with the parents in the living room. The Vue family came to the United States about seven years ago. Mr. Vue spoke very little English. He was very angry about the welfare system that was supposed to be helping him. I asked him to calm down and we explained the reasons why we came to see him. He indicated that he was not able to participate in the Employment Training because of his consistent back pain from a war injury. Back in Laos, he served as an artillery soldier for the United States Alliance during the Vietnam War in the 1960s and early 1970s. He was given the job of sabotaging the road used by the North Vietnamese army, which was located in both Laos and South Vietnam. He was injured two times. To this day he still has nightmares and flashbacks about the war. Due to the suspension of his public assistance benefits, he did not have enough money to buy food and clothing for his children. Most of the time his children would go to school hungry. Lastly, he also had a difficult time adapting and assimilating to the American society.

Approaches Towards Helping the Client:

I thanked Mr. Vue for sharing his powerful story. I had great sympathy for the Vue family, especially all the things that were happening to them. There were several approaches that I used to intervene with this family. First, I tried to build rapport with the Vue family. I wanted to convey empathy and understanding of their circumstances. Winning their trust would open up their communication. Second, I identified the resources this family needed, and served as a broker in connecting the family with these resources. For instance, I contacted the Salvation Army for food and clothing for the family; referred Mr. Vue to a mental health counselor for his depression; and took the family to see a caseworker in order to apply for Food Stamps, Medical Assistance, and W-2 benefits. Third, I worked closely with the family's caseworker to monitor their progress. Finally, I helped Mr. Vue to understand that he either needed to enter a work training program, or apply for the Supplemental Security Income (SSI) program if his chronic back pain and other health problems prevented him from obtaining employment.

Outcomes:

As time evolved, Mr. Vue and his family have come to have a greater understanding about the policies in our welfare system. He was willing to work part-time, and still see his counselor once every two weeks. He was diagnosed as having Posttraumatic Stress Disorder and continues to see his mental health counselor. After several months had passed, he was declared eligible to receive Supplemental Security Income (SSI), as it was determined that his health problems would preclude him from obtaining gainful employment. In working with this family, I had to be very sensitive about their cultural norms. Family loyalty in the Hmong culture is so strong that anyone who goes against the wishes of the family is very likely to be ex-communicated from the family. For a Hmong to live without the support of one's family is to live in disgrace in the Hmong society. Other Hmong people will not respect a person if they know that the person's own family no longer respects him/her. Therefore, reputation is a key factor in working with Hmong clients.

In conclusion, this case is an example of the many cases that I worked with at my field placement. I have empowered many clients to make positive changes in their lives. In order to work successfully with clients, we have to show empathy, caring, and understanding of their issues. We must be able to listen, reflect, probe the appropriate questions, and work with clients to assist them in making positive changes. In addition, we need to understand and respect their cultural values.

Questions for Students:

Identify the needs of Mr. Vue and his family. How did the social worker seek to empower Mr. Vue and his family members? Specify some of the Hmong cultural values that are illustrated in this case example. What evidence is there that the social worker and the Vue family members viewed Mr. Vue as the primary decision maker in this family? Do the actions of the social worker and the other family members suggest that the Hmong culture views the father as the "head" of the family? If you were the social worker for the Vue family, would you have done differently? Would you have sought to convey to Mr. And Mrs. Vue (and to the children) that Mr. And Mrs. Vue <u>should</u> have an egalitarian relationship? If you took this latter approach, what are the likely consequences in the way in which the various Vue family members would relate to you?

Chapter 13: Sexism and Efforts for Achieving Equality

Changing Domestic Violence Legislation
Janet M. Wright, Ph.D., MSW

Credentials:

Ph.D. in Social Work
Currently Associate Professor and Chairperson of a University Social Work Department

Case Example:

In the late 1970s, there were still laws on the books in some states that allowed husbands to beat their wives under certain conditions. As a recent MSW graduate, I was working as a drug abuse counselor but I was also meeting with a group of helping professionals and women who had personal experience with or connections to domestic violence. We were strategizing how to provide services for the battered women we were seeing in our work and in our friends' and neighbors' homes. We surmised that they were merely the tip of the iceberg.

By staffing a hotline with volunteers in a windowless, broom closet donated as an office in a church, we were able to gather some limited data. Ninety-five percent of the women who called needed shelter. Feeling helpless, some of us offered our homes as safe houses. That data, shocking as it was limited, convinced The United Way to grant us start up money, $11,000. A year later we had grants totaling over $100,000, a rented shelter, and a staff of six. I became one of those staff members.

But it wasn't enough. The women who came to the shelter and the women who called shared their frightening stories and a theme began to emerge. Restraining orders were not only useless, they were dangerous—because they gave false security. A woman could get a restraining order against her abuser, but it didn't protect her. She could wave it in front of the police when they found her battered and bloodied and all they could do was to tell her to take her abuser to court—which could take weeks or even months. Once in court, the batterer might simply be told, like a naughty child, not to do that again. It was a worthless paper.

We had to change legislation so that the restraining order would have some enforcement behind it. We supported a law that would allow the police to arrest the abuser when the survivor had a restraining order and pressed charges. We were able to find sponsors for the bill, but we knew we had to draw in more attention and support if we wanted it to be taken seriously. What would create the biggest impact? What had grabbed our attention as workers? Of course, it was the women's stories! The stories of shaking the restraining orders in the abuser's face as he laughed and broke down the door and held a gun to his partner's head as her children watched. The legislators needed to hear the raw human cost of the ineffectual present law.

And so we helped the women, some living in the shelter, some not, to prepare. We asked them to write their stories, then tell them, to practice. Meanwhile, we called the bill's sponsors, got the names of legislators that were likely to support the bill and those (many) who were on the fence. We felt it was important for the women to be successful in this venture—to feel support. So we ignored those legislators who were outspoken against the bill.

We invited the media. Having made contacts in the past, we invited TV and newspaper reporters who, we knew, understood the dynamics of woman abuse and were eager to share and to increase their knowledge.

And the women continued to rehearse their stories.

Finally, the day arrived. We were fifteen or twenty women with babies in strollers and toddlers in hand. We toddled, rolled, and nervously strode into the Capitol where we had reserved a room (to make it easy for the legislators to get there). The media was there. The legislators straggled in—first five, then 10, then 20. The women stood in a semi-circle and one-by-one told their stories of how the restraining order had failed them. It took only half an hour. There was a moment of pregnant silence. Some of the women were weeping. Some of the legislators had tears in their eyes. And then the silence was broken, as legislators, in their tailored suits and silken ties, reached out to the women, in their free clothes from the YWCA clothes closet. The women beamed as they were congratulated and respectfully questioned. The TV cameras kept rolling.

The bill passed. Several years later a second bill was passed which instituted mandatory arrests whenever there is a battery. This means that the survivor no longer must press charges her(him)self—the police must arrest the abuser.

That day, fifteen women reclaimed their dignity, their respect, and their power through their voices. And twenty legislators got in touch again with their humanity.

Questions for Students:

This case example from the late 1970s and early 1980s used the strategy of having persons affected (in this case battered women) meet with legislators with media present. How are women currently being oppressed or discriminated against in our society? What current legislative changes need to be made today to better empower women who are being discriminated against or oppressed? What other strategies might be used to advocate for legislative changes to better empower women who are victims of oppression and discrimination?

Chapter 14: Aging and Gerontological Services

Using "Validation" and "Reality Orientation" with a Person with Dementia
Erin King

Credentials:

Currently I am a social work intern, finishing my last few hours at my field placement. When I am done with my internship I will graduate with a Bachelor's degree in Social Work. My field placement is at a nursing home.

Case Example:

One of the four units, or wings, at the nursing home is primarily reserved for residents with Dementia. Dementia impairs many functions of the brain, one of them being short-term memory, which causes the most recent memories in a person's mind to be erased. A person who has Dementia typically talks about experiences that happened in their past as if they are happening at that moment, because that is what they remember. When communicating with a person who has Dementia, it is important for the listener to realize that the things the person is talking about may seem like "nonsense" because they are not congruent with the environment in which the person with Dementia is currently living. However, these things actually make sense to the person with Dementia because in her mind, a resident may believe that she is in another place or another time in her life. Two techniques that the staff employees use when communicating with residents with Dementia are Validation and Reality Orientation.

Validation is demonstrated by listening to everything that the person with Dementia has to say, without correcting the inconsistencies. Allowing the person to talk about what she sees, feels, and hears, by prompting her with questions about specific characteristics as well as detail, will help that person to feel comfortable and to know that she is being heard and understood. It can be upsetting to a person with Dementia to be told that what she is thinking is not actually real. To someone with Dementia, whatever she sees and thinks in her mind seems real and telling her otherwise is even more confusing for the person. Asking the person to give details about what person, feeling, or object she may be talking about allows the person to keep her dignity because she won't feel that she has "lost her mind."

Reality Orientation is used when the listener patiently explains to the person with Dementia the time, place, people around them, and what is going on, when the person is confused about her environment. It helps the person with Dementia to differentiate between what is real and what may be in the past or not be real at all.

One particular resident that I have spent a lot of time with during my field placement has a diagnosis of Dementia with Alzheimer's disease, as well as deteriorating eyesight. "Mabel," as I'll call her, gets very confused about the activities that go on around her. One afternoon as I was passing through the unit that Mabel lives on, I noticed that she was walking around the unit and appeared to be very confused and puzzled. I asked her where she was headed and she replied, "I'd like to go home but I can't seem to remember how to get out of here." I attempted to use Reality Orientation in my reply to her by gently reminding her where she was and that her family knows where she is. "Mabel, you have a room down the hall; it's decorated with your things. Your niece and nephew know you're here and they come to visit you every week." She seemed surprised to hear this information and requested to see her room, so I offered to take her down the hall to show her the room.

Once we were in Mabel's room, I asked her about the pictures that she has in frames, sitting on a shelf. She replied, "Oh, I don't know about those, I can't see them. But have you seen the one's in the living room?" I told her that no, I had not seen them, but could she describe them to me. She proceeded to describe the paintings, done by her husband, that were in the living room, according to Mabel, just down the hall. She couldn't remember too many details about them, but she knew she was talking about her husband and her home. By using Validation I helped her to recall and to enjoy the comfort of her memories by allowing her to tell me about the paintings that had obviously meant so much to her. The fact that we were standing in a nursing home, rather than her own living room, was an irrelevant fact so I did not feel the need to point it out to her because I did not want to upset her.

The conversation turned back to the pictures that Mabel has in her room. Due to poor eyesight Mabel could only see the shape of the picture frames; she had no idea what they were of and who was in them. I began to describe the pictures in great detail, from the color and style of the hair of the people pictured, to the minute details of their clothes, the positions they were in, the background, the sky, weather, and setting of the pictures. As the scene was painted in Mabel's mind, her face lit up and she was able to recall these precious mementoes of happy times in her life. Mabel and I had looked at each and every picture in her room. I described every detail that I saw in the pictures, and Mabel shared every detail that she remembered in her mind. Together we shared many smiles and laughs, and before we were done, Mabel exclaimed, "I'm so happy that now when I look at these pictures in here, I'll know exactly what they're showing!"

By using both Validation and Reality Orientation when I communicated with Mabel on this particular occasion, I helped her to keep her dignity by not embarrassing her when she was confused about her surroundings. Mabel was able to feel comfortable sharing her personal stories with me about her own home and the special people in her life. When Mabel felt frustrated about her poor eyesight, I helped her to find a way to see her pictures again.

Questions for Students:

Describe Validation and Reality Orientation. In what ways are each of these concepts consistent with empowerment? What did this social work intern do to demonstrate Validation and to demonstrate Reality Orientation? Assume you are a person with dementia living in a nursing home—what special needs are you apt to have? What other services need to be provided by social workers to meet these special needs?

Chapter 15: Health Problems and Medical Social Services

Extended Family Therapy for a Stress-Impacted Youth
Joel Ambelang, MSSW

Credentials:
Master of Science, School of Social Work,
Currently, Director of the University Baccalaureate Social Work Program

Case Example:

Several years ago I was a clinical social worker at a private clinic that provided individual and family therapy and assessment.

Bobby, a white male, age 10, was referred by his pediatrician. His mother had taken him to the physician because of frequent somatic complaints, stomachache, headache, and frequent colds. He was failing in school, and his behavior featured agitation, poor attention span, oppositional behaviors in school and at home. He was referred for an evaluation. At the intake session, mother discussed her frustration with Bobby, his negative attitude, lack of cooperation, and "pestering."

Bobby's mother had been divorced from the father for about two years. Bobby, his mother, and a younger sister live in a three-bedroom duplex, with another woman and her daughter. Bobby's father remarried and has a one-year-old child and an infant with his present wife. Bobby has weekend visits with his father. His mother reports that after each of these visits, Bobby's behavior features more acting out. He vacillates between agitation and withdrawal. He does not complete his homework and refuses to participate in the classroom. Bobby was referred to his pediatrician for a complete physical to rule out any medical conditions which may be contributing to his behavior. We arranged weekly appointments for 90 minutes each with three units in each session that would address the dyad of Bobby and his mother, Bobby alone, and his mother alone. As the assessment process unfolded it became increasingly apparent that Bobby was reacting to the stress and conflict of his parents' divorce and the subsequent living arrangements that threatened his relationship with his mother and father. The woman with whom they live played the role of surrogate parent with Bobby, which he resents. The mutual childcare arrangement worked for the mothers, but did not work for the children. When Bobby would visit his father on weekends, the loss Bobby experienced with his parents' divorce and the unresolved issues of his parents' emotional abandonment, the chaos of living with a comparative stranger whom Bobby felt was an intruder into his relationship with his mother, the lack of emotional and physical boundaries of this blended system, the lack of nurturance from his mother who was dealing with her own career and financial stressors, the lack of order and predictability in his life all led to a social environment that was chaotic and disorganized. Bobby needed consistency, coherence, predictability, emotional and social support, and a sense of belonging.

The plan was to meet once a week with Bobby and his mother until they had restored a measure of mutual trust and a sense of belonging in their relationship. The next step was to incorporate the woman and her 8-year-old daughter, with whom Bobby and his mother lived, into the helping process. We formulated concrete behaviors that would help Bobby feel a part of their shared system. A primary behavior was the adults to validate Bobby's feelings and listen to what he had to say. He developed somatic complaints, had withdrawn and acted out, because he felt emotionally and socially isolated. Others were so occupied with their own issues that they ignored Bobby. Bobby used a mood cube to indicate his feelings on a daily basis. His mother particularly was to acknowledge his feelings and encourage him to talk about his feelings. It was important for all concerned to recognize feelings and verbally express them.

When the household members reached a point that showed constructive, positive behaviors toward Bobby and each other, we expanded the therapy circle to include Bobby's father and his wife. We initially met with Bobby's father and his wife to define and agree on the issues and to further define how they could help Bobby feel a part of a biological and blended family that lived in two households. It became apparent that there were many unresolved issues between Mom and Dad. It was necessary to meet with them as a divorced couple to develop a focus on Bobby as the client. Whatever their issues with each other, the important focus was to help Bobby in specific areas of his social, emotional, and intellectual development. They must be a team with one purpose, setting aside their issues with each other. The next phase was to hold joint sessions with Bobby, his mother, and his father. Again the focus was on Bobby's sense of belonging, validating his feelings, attending to his school performance by participating together in school conferences and sharing responsibility for monitoring and discussing his homework. In each of these steps, the participants were given specific tasks to help them help one another with communication of feelings and affirmation for one another and Bobby. This phase involved 20 weekly sessions.

The final phase was to have three biweekly sessions with all significant others which included Bobby, his mother, his sister, his father and his wife, and the mother's "roommate." These sessions, designed with stringent guidelines and structure to maintain the sense of purpose, produced a common understanding of Bobby's needs, a common strategy to meet those needs, and a daily measure of how each viewed progress through meetings to discuss the day. Those meetings were structured to exclude all extraneous matters and distractions. It was their time to monitor their social and emotional status and its affect on the family system, with emphasis on Bobby's emotional and behavioral responses. There were three 90-minute conjoint sessions.

We had follow-up sessions with Bobby and his parents every three weeks for about three months and then monthly sessions. After one of the monthly sessions, the family agreed that they no longer needed to meet. About one year later we received a letter from Bobby's mother saying that his school year had been a success. He was getting A's and B's in school. There were no more somatic complaints. The mother moved into a place of her own and Bobby continued to see his father on weekly visits. When Bobby felt that he had some control in his life, that his social environment was more orderly and predictable, that he belonged, he thrived.

Questions for Students:

Summarize the somatic, psychological, social, and educational difficulties that Bobby was experiencing. Assume you are Bobby in this case example; what would you be feeling and needing (living in two different family systems with the biological parents having ongoing conflicts) before family therapy was provided? What empowerment strategies were used to intervene with

Bobby? If you were the social worker assigned to work with Bobby, what would you have done differently?

Chapter 16: Physical and Mental Disabilities and Rehabilitation

Empowering an Individual with Cerebral Palsy
Kathy (Kinner) Klika, BSW

Credentials:

BSW

Currently I am the Admissions Director at an agency that provides residential services to more than five hundred individuals with developmental disabilities, mental illness, physical disabilities, and traumatic brain injuries. An array of individualized residential options are provided, including supervised apartments, adult family homes, group homes and supportive home care.

Empowerment for individuals with disabilities involves providing needed assistance while honoring choice. This requires asking questions and taking the time to listen to responses, both verbal and nonverbal. Creativity, flexibility, and a willingness to allow risk are all essential.

Case Example:

Mary is an intelligent and independent woman with cerebral palsy. She uses a wheelchair and is transferred with a mechanical lift. Mary has some swallowing difficulties and eats a mechanical soft diet that she feeds herself with an adapted spoon. Due to significant contractures and spasticity, Mary requires complete assistance with all areas of daily living including bathing, dressing, toileting, health care, medication monitoring, food preparation and housekeeping. Because of her cerebral palsy, Mary's speech is very difficult to understand. She chooses to communicate mainly through the use of a touch talker where she types in her thoughts, letter by letter, and then relays the communication through a synthesized voice.

Mary was referred to our agency by her county case manager. She had been living in an apartment with the assistance of live-in staff who had just resigned. Mary had experienced many changes in her support staff during the ten years that she lived in the apartment and often felt that she was at their mercy as it related to her cares and schedule. Consequently, she was looking to move to a more reliable living situation. When I first met Mary I was immediately struck by her wit and determination. As I was asking her questions regarding her preferences and care needs, her case manager, Jan, rather than waiting for Mary to type in her response, began to answer questions for her. Sensing Mary's frustration, I awaited her reply. She typed feverously and pressed the button on her touch talker which related in a commanding synthesized voice, "Thank you Jan, for your vote of confidence." Mary and I smiled at each other, and Jan stopped answering the questions for Mary. Mary and I had a long conversation about the services that would be provided at the group home that she was considering. Mary already knew some of the people who live at the home and following a visit for dinner, decided to move.

Mary's choices and preferences are valued. As part of the transition to her new home, Mary was asked to train each staff member on the nuances of her care. She continues to train new staff members at the home. Mary is encouraged to discuss concerns directly with the staff and knows that management is available to intervene if necessary. Feedback from Mary and her housemates are incorporated into employee performance reviews.

Mary is presented with options related to her health and makes informed choices. At one time, serious medical problems necessitated a colostomy and gastric tube for feeding. The tube feedings were discontinued when Mary regained her strength. Despite conventional wisdom, Mary was determined to have the colostomy reversed as well. After being provided with all of the information including benefits, risks and possible complications, Mary chose to wait several months and then proceed with the reversal surgery. The surgery was ultimately successful. With the assistance of an attorney advocate, Mary has drafted a last will and testament and advance directives for healthcare.

Despite her physical limitations, Mary is determined to earn an income. With the assistance of caregivers, she has developed a creative job that allows for some additional income. She attends a day program part time and also sells cards, wrapping paper and gift items that are delivered from a wholesaler to her home. Mary always has a supply of products hanging in a bag on her wheelchair and is known to "wheel and deal" with her friends and associates. These sales provide Mary with some discretionary income. Mary is a savvy consumer and the stores that she frequents view her as a valued and respected customer.

Mary is an active participant in her community. She is assisted in arranging for transportation using a specialized van service or the group home van. She chooses her activities and has many friends. Favorites include trips to the mall, movies, church, visiting with friends, and occasional trips to the casino. One night, upon returning from the casino, Mary was asked how she did. With a smirk on her face she typed into her touch talker, "I lost my ass!"

Mary is interested in issues that affect people with disabilities, and participates actively in the political process. She attends political forums, provides feedback to candidates on issues, wears political buttons, and has never missed an opportunity to vote.

Through her own determination and the assistance of a dedicated team of professionals, Mary has been empowered to lead a full and active life in the community.

Questions for Students:

Describe the physical disabilities (associated with cerebral palsy) that Mary has. Assume you are Mary—what would you be feeling, and what would be your needs? How did the staff at this agency (including the group home component) seek to empower Mary to constructively meet the challenges (including physical, emotional, and social) she encountered? If you were the social worker for Mary, what would you have done differently? What other services would currently be beneficial for Mary?

Chapter 17: Overpopulation, Misuse of the Environment, and Family Planning

Empowering a Client to Make a Decision
Jessica Hornik, BSW

Credentials:

BSW, December 2002

I am a social work intern at a high school. Part of our ideology here is that a student cannot learn to their fullest if they are dealing with social and emotional problems. The school social workers are here to help students deal with some of their issues. Most services here are utilized on a voluntary basis, although we sometimes do get referrals from other staff at the high school. Some of the services that we provide include: both individual and group counseling, teen parents support services, and resources referrals to outside community committees and organizations.

Case Example:

I first met Melissa Michaels, 14, on my second day of my field placement. She walked into my office and I asked her to take a seat (which she did so, but with much disdain). She was my first student that I saw during placement and I hadn't been told much about her before our first meeting face to face. She was an incoming freshman who the middle school counselors advised us to see based on her mother's concern for her. The girl that sat in front of me was obviously physically mature for her age. She was average height with a bigger build. Her black leather-clad legs were extended in front of her while she slouched in her chair. She was fair skinned which set off her black bobbed hair even more. Her face was clean of all makeup except for her black lined eyes. A spiked collar surrounded her neck and she crossed her arms over her ripped black tee shirt. Her face showed little expression, but her body language talked for her. She appeared to be a hardened girl who was covering up a lot of hurt. My guess was that she just needed to be loved and cared for. Over the next few months, I would find out just how true my guess would be.

That first meeting Melissa and I were able to muddle through with minimal difficulty. I could see in her eyes and in her demeanor that she didn't believe I could understand her story. Here I was a young college-educated, pastel-clad, intern just 8 years older than her, and she a struggling high school, gothic-clad student, who had probably lived more than I had in just her 14 years. Slowly but surely she opened up and I was able to find out a little bit about her. She told me that her parents were still married and living together, although she didn't live with them. Her parents lived in low income housing in the "bad" part of town. Her brother was in his twenties and lived out of state. She talked a lot about the things she was interested in; old cars and sketching. That first session I was able to see a glimpse of her life; she didn't get along with her parents and tried to spend as much time away from home as possible.

I met with Melissa weekly and it took a few more meetings like the first before I felt like she was connecting with me enough to open up and be able to trust me. As with many of the incoming 9th grade students, I began seeing Melissa for no specific reason or issue, but rather as a support person. After the first few sessions I was able to see that Melissa was needing someone to really love and care about her. Since she really disliked being at home, she spent most of her time over at her friend Tracy's apartment. Tracy lived with her mother and her apartment was also close to Melissa's parents' house. Tracy and Melissa were very close, spending a lot of their time together. So much so that Melissa mentioned she stayed most nights at Tracy's apartment. I soon found out that her friend wasn't a very good influence to have around but their friendship was where Melissa was receiving her love and support. Tracy's mom couldn't pay her bills, so random men came and went from Tracy's apartment and helped to pay the rent. Tracy and her mother also practiced witchcraft which Melissa was becoming interested in. Since Melissa didn't feel that she received any love and support from her parents, she found it in Tracy's seemingly unconditional friendship and support.

As the semester progressed I could see the rapport between Melissa and I start to grow. She no longer "hated" coming to talk to me. Although Melissa never commented on it, she alluded to the idea that Tracy and herself were "partying" and I suspected drug or at least alcohol use between the girls. My concern for Melissa grew. She was a smart girl with lots of potential and concerned parents, which is more than a lot of kids I see have. I was worried that Melissa would get sucked in by Tracy's lifestyle and get stuck in a predicament that she couldn't get herself out of. Halfway through the semester I found out through other staff at the high school that Tracy was pregnant. When Melissa came in to talk to me soon afterwards (she had ignored my passes for a month) I noticed a marked difference in her look and attitude. Her hair was no longer black but a softer brown. Her clothes weren't all dark colored but she wore jeans and a simple shirt instead. Although she still had skulls drawn on her arms, she no longer wore the spiked collar. She smiled and made eye contact with me. Something had undoubtedly changed with her in the last 4 weeks. She told me she hadn't come in to see me because life had been busy. Tracy and she fought and ended their friendship. Her relationship with her parents had taken a turn for the better when they moved into a different apartment and she was able to have her own bedroom with a lock! But obviously most exciting to her was a new boyfriend that her parents approved of. We talked that session (and many afterwards) about her boyfriend and how close they had become. We talked about Tracy and her pregnancy. Melissa was disappointed with her friend who had become pregnant while she was drunk at a party.

This year at the high school we have 11 girls who are pregnant or parenting. I work with these girls in a teen parent group where we supply education and support. Through working with these girls I have learned a few things. One, I have gained a multitude of knowledge on birth control and other parenting concepts. The other thing that I've learned is that 7th and 8th graders are having sexual intercourse and it's never too early to talk about birth control options with a child. My concern with Melissa was that she still needed love and support so badly and I worried that she would use sexual intercourse with her new boyfriend as a way to fulfill those needs. I asked Melissa if her and her boyfriend were having sex, or had talked about it. Her face turned red and she told me that they had talked about having sex but hadn't done anything yet. In the same conversation we had also talked about how Tracy was going to possibly give her baby up for adoption and how Melissa disapproved of the whole issue. We talked about how she didn't want to end up pregnant like her friend.

Strategies used with the client:

After having met with Melissa several times and learning about her situation, I found it appropriate to bring up birth control with her. She told me that if her and her boyfriend would have sex that they would probably use condoms. I agreed that that was a good method especially for preventing STDs and AIDS. I informed her that sometimes condoms were inconvenient and easy to forget about in the heat of the moment. I also told her that there are many different forms of birth control available to her and they could be obtained through Planned Parenthood (of which there was a nearby center). I let her know that the services were confidential and inexpensive. At this point she told me that she was not interested in anything at the moment. I explained to her that it was not my place to push her to use a form of birth control but instead it was between her and her partner. Before our session ended I let her know that when and if she was ready to make the decision to use another form of birth control (other than using condoms) that I would be here for support. As she left I gave her the number for Planned Parenthood and hoped that she would use it.

At the end of our first session together I let her know that I would be there for her to chat with and help work through issues in her life as they came up. I explained to her that my services as a school social worker were to support her, be a sounding board for her, advocate for her, and help her obtain any resources she needed. I also asked her if she would like to continue seeing me and she said that yes she would. We agreed on a weekly basis, but if something came up, it was all right for her to not come in. (Since there were no pressing issues this arrangement worked out fine.) Her involvement was entirely voluntary.

Throughout my sessions with Melissa, I never once told her what to do or gave her my opinion. I always let her know that I was there to support her in whatever she choose, but it was her life and she would live with the outcomes of her decisions. My intentions were to make sure she knew where she could get information and make sure she knew someone would be there to educate, support, guide and help her to assess what she wanted, but I always made it clear I could not make the final decision for her.

Outcome:

It had been quite a few weeks since I had met with Melissa when on her own she stopped by to see me one day. She had never done this before, so I knew that something must be up. I told her to come in and have a seat and asked her what was up. She asked me if I remembered telling her that if she were ever ready to go on birth control to come up and see me. I told her that I did remember. She informed me that both her and her boyfriend had decided that they were ready to have sex and she wanted more information on what was available at Planned Parenthood and how to access it. I told her a little bit about the different forms of birth control. She said that she had looked into the patch a little bit because she had seen it on television as being a new form of birth control that was available. She also said that she had called to find out what the hours of the Planned Parenthood center were and if she would have to make an appointment. She was told that she could keep things confidential and her parents would not have to find out that she was sexually active. She wanted to know what the gynecological exam was all about and I was able to help ease her fears and give her some information on what would take place and why she needed one. A problem arose as far as transportation was concerned since I could not legally transport her myself; we talked about other ways in which she could get to her appointment. She also told me that her boyfriend wanted to meet with me as well to talk about their different options concerning birth control.

Melissa let me know that it felt good to have someone to be able to talk openly about sex issues with, because she felt comfortable that I wouldn't judge her. She felt empowered to make her own adult decision about sex and birth control based on our sessions together. Hooking her up with outside resources and information helped to get the conversation going with her and her boyfriend and make them feel like they could address the issues they needed to, to prevent pregnancy and STDs.

Summary:

Family planning is based on respect for yourself and your partner. It takes a mature and proactive client to make the move to obtain birth control. Throughout my sessions with Melissa I gave her the control to lead the sessions where she wanted them to go. Deciding to have sex and deal with any consequences that may come as a result, is a mature adult decision and I wanted her to feel empowered to make her own responsible safe decision. In my eyes, despite her tender age of 14, I saw and respected her as an adult making adult decisions and soon she saw herself the same way. I gave her the information she needed and let her know that my door was always open if she needed to talk. At times I was worried that her need for love and affection would win out with her boyfriend and she wouldn't respect herself enough to make the initiative to use birth control. In cases like this all we can do is give our clients the tools they need to make a good informed decision, and hope they use them. Thankfully Melissa did.

Questions for Students:

What strategies did this social work intern use to develop rapport with Melissa, so that Melissa eventually felt comfortable in discussing the issues she was facing? Assume you are Melissa—how would you feel about: being distant from your parents; dressing in dark, gothic clothing; and confused about whether to be sexually active? If you were the social worker for Melissa, what would you have done differently? Do you believe it is desirable and ethical for school social workers to refer 14-year-old clients who are considering becoming sexually active to Planned Parenthood? Why, or why not?

Chapter 17: Overpopulation, Misuse of the Environment, and Family Planning

Empowering a Pregnant Sixteen-Year-Old Teenager and Her Parents
Debra S. Borquist, MSSW

Credentials:

BA, Psychology
MSSW
Licensed Social Worker
Lecturer (full-time), at a University Social Work Department

Case Example:

In 1999 I was working as a Case Manager in an agency whose mission was to assist children with severe mental health issues to remain in their homes and community. Historically, many children with severe mental health issues have been removed from their homes and often placed in institutions. This program used a strength-based wrap-around approach to supporting children and families. The program was funded by diverted funds that would generally be used to pay for out of home and institutional placement.

Client problem: (Multiple issues—Focus on family planning)

I began working with a young woman named LaRita, 16, and her family in the spring of 1999. LaRita was two months pregnant and very unsure about her options and future plans. In addition, LaRita had previously been diagnosed with depression and had been referred to our program due to a pending delinquency charge (for a fight at school). The District Attorney was recommending that LaRita be placed at a child caring institution for a period of six months. LaRita and her family wanted her to remain at home and to make a decision regarding her pregnancy.

Services:

I initially made arrangements to meet the family at their home. The parents were very upset and LaRita was initially very quiet. I met with the family to explain our agency mission and philosophy. I explained that it was not my job to tell them what to do or to direct them to particular services, but rather to explore their family strengths and needs and to assist them in creating an individualized plan.

During our first few meetings I talked with LaRita and her parents regarding a number of areas, including school, home life, employment, family culture and history, religion, family relationships, the pregnancy, and so on. I then completed a Strengths and Needs Assessment with the family to assist in recognizing what was going well in the family and what areas needed to be addressed.

After gathering basic information about the current situation, I began asking the family about their strengths and LaRita's individual strengths. Initially it was difficult for the parents to answer my questions. They were currently not feeling like very good parents and they were very disappointed in their daughter's behaviors. When families are in crisis it is often very difficult for them to identify their strengths, yet every family has them. As a social worker it is very important to understand this and to assist families to focus on their strengths, as they are building blocks towards the future. I could see their struggle in answering my questions and began to talk with them about their family history and culture. They were able to talk about challenging times that they had been through in the past and were able to discuss how they managed to get through those times. They soon began to identify many of their family strengths. For example, despite the fact that they had struggled with discussing the topic of sex, they were able to identify that they were a close family with a long history of strong family ties. They were very familiar with the mental health system for children and were strong advocates for LaRita. They also had dreams that their daughter would have a happy life and perhaps even attend college.

In terms of family needs, the parents indicated an immediate need for strategies to talk with their daughter more openly regarding her current pregnancy and future birth control issues. They indicated that they had both been raised in homes where sex was not openly discussed and thus, they had a difficult time talking with LaRita about these issues. They had hoped to be more open with her and were now feeling like failures given her unplanned pregnancy.

After discussing the multiple family strengths and needs, we focused on LaRita. After much discussion, the family was able to identify a number of LaRita's strengths. They indicated that she was a bright young woman who had historically done well in school. LaRita indicated that she was also very artistic and enjoyed music. LaRita had struggled with mental health issues for a number of years and the family was able to identify a number of coping strategies. In addition, they had relatives in the area and LaRita had a close relationship with a special (paternal) aunt. They were able to identify that at the time of the referral to our agency, LaRita's mental health issues were fairly stable. She was involved with an excellent therapist and had been consistently taking her medications. She was enrolled in public school and had a number of friends. All of these strengths were identified by LaRita and her parents and were reported to the Court as reasons why LaRita's needs were best served in her parental home and in her own community.

As a team (LaRita, her parents, and me) we identified the following needs: LaRita needed assistance in a number of areas including employment, anger management, and education regarding family planning and her choices. Her parents admitted that they had been reluctant to talk with LaRita regarding her pregnancy. They felt guilty and frustrated. LaRita indicated that she had not intended to get pregnant and was very nervous and embarrassed. This was clearly a difficult time for the family. Despite the turmoil, the parents were very clear that they wanted their daughter to remain in their home.

Using the strengths of the family and providing a clear plan to the Courts, we were able to successfully convince the Courts to allow LaRita to remain in her parental home. At the same time we began to address LaRita's pregnancy and family communication.

I discussed with the family a number of options regarding our next steps. The family and I created a plan to meet the needs of both LaRita and her family by utilizing their many strengths. In terms of LaRita's pregnancy, the family decided that family counseling would be helpful to address their issues of communication (specifically regarding LaRita's pregnancy). The family indicated that they were very comfortable working with me and that they were hoping that I would supply the family counseling. I explained that I was also very comfortable with them, but that family counseling was outside of my role. I told them I knew a number of excellent family therapists in the community and that I could make a referral. I also encouraged them to talk with their family minister and LaRita's counselor for additional referrals. I wanted them to clearly understand that the decision regarding their provider was in their hands. They indicated that they were surprised in my approach and stated they had worked with many "social services types." They told me they were used to people telling them what *their* goals *should* be and which provider they would have to see. I made it very clear that these decisions were for them to make and that I could provide information about ideas and services, but that I would not be imposing any decisions. Given their level of comfort and their request for my close involvement, we agreed that they would attend two to three family sessions and that we would meet together after each session to check in and to discuss the family's progress.

We also made plans for LaRita, her parents, and me, to meet with a local family planning agency. Again, this was a family decision. With my assistance, they explored local family planning agencies and picked the one they believed was best for them. LaRita identified that she wanted her parents to be more involved in helping her to make her decision but felt uncomfortable about making her decisions, but had felt too nervous to initiate communication in this area. The agency they chose provided a neutral environment and key information and education regarding issues of adoption, abortion, and birth control.

LaRita and her family received the information regarding her options and the family counseling provided the skills to discuss their issues. We discussed the information at a subsequent family meeting. LaRita's parents told her that they would support her no matter what she decided to do but that it needed to be her decision.

Outcome:

During the next twelve weeks, I met with the family on a weekly basis. They were clearly making progress towards better communication and decision-making. LaRita ultimately decided to have her child adopted by a couple who she believed were better prepared for a child at this time. With her parents' support, the family planning education, and ongoing communication with her parents, LaRita was able to make this difficult decision. She believed her decision was best for her child and for herself.

LaRita indicated she felt good about her ability to make her own life decisions and her parents appreciated that their family was able to create the intervention plan that best suited their needs, while taking into account the strengths of their family. LaRita indicated that this experience had helped her define her goals, hopes, and dreams. She aspired to graduate from high school and attend college. She also indicated that although she was not currently sexually active, she was planning to utilize birth control in the future. LaRita's parents indicated that were proud of their daughter's decision and that they were more comfortable talking with her about her decision, life choices, and her future plans.

Questions for Students:

What strategies did this Case Manager use to seek to empower LaRita and her parents to make decisions about LaRita's pregnancy, and for LaRita to set some future life goals? Assume you are LaRita—how would you feel about being sixteen years old, depressed, and having mental health issues? If you were the Case Manager for LaRita, what would you have done differently? If you were the Case Manager for LaRita, would you have encouraged her to seek an abortion? Why, or why not? The profession of social work has taken a pro-choice position on the abortion issue. Are you supportive of the pro-choice position? Why, or why not? If the Case Manager for LaRita would have held strong pro-life views, do you think he or she should have referred the case to someone who has pro-choice views? Why, or why not?